S0-AGU-253

New York is a food city and eateries of all kinds are found right in our neighborhood. There's an abundance of dining choices from Irish pubs, pizzerias and steakhouses, to fine dining, breweries, delicatessens and a vast array of ethnic cuisines.

Madison Square Garden, The World's Most Famous Arena, is located a few blocks away from the Empire State Building. Home to the New York Knicks, the New York Rangers, and the New York Liberty, Madison Square Garden is the ultimate sports arena for fans and players alike.

TOP: Midtown Manhattan is viewed from the Williamsburg Bridge, which crosses the East River and connects the Lower East Side of Manhattan with the Williamsburg neighborhood of Brooklyn. BOTTOM LEFT: Standing in the center of Manhattan, ESB is easily visible. This is the view from Madison Square Park. BOTTOM RIGHT: ESB is glimpsed through the arch in Washington Square Park. Located at the foot of Fifth Avenue, it is a landmark in the Manhattan neighborhood of Greenwich Village. PAGE 13: A view of ESB looking northwest, with the Hudson River in the background.

Welcome

Lawrence A. Wien (left) in 1961, is handed a model of the Empire State Building by Colonel Henry Crown, Chicago industrialist (center), and Louis R. Menagh, president of Prudential Insurance Company (right, holding check), at the closing of the purchase of ESB.

Peter L. Malkin

From Peter L. Malkin
Empire State Building Company L.L.C.

On behalf of Empire State Building Company L.L.C., welcome to the Empire State Building! These words have greeted visitors for 80 years and we continue the tradition today.

We are so pleased that you have decided to visit our international icon. When you first see the Empire State Building in New York City, you become part of its magic, history, and the dreams it has inspired for generations. You cannot help being touched from the moment you set foot in our Landmarked Art Deco lobby and experience the breathtaking, panoramic views from the 86th and 102nd floor Observatories. Whether you are a first time visitor, returning with children or grandchildren, or even proposing marriage, this is The Real Magic, The Real New York.

I have been involved with the care and preservation of this iconic building since 1961 when my father-in-law Lawrence A. Wien, Harry B. Helmsley, and I acquired a long-term lease on the Empire State Building. Then, in 2001, I arranged for the purchase of the land, bringing ownership of the entire building together for the first time since 1951. As stewards for the building, Empire State Building Company L.L.C., ensures that this state-of-the-art international treasure will be enjoyed for generations to come.

Today, the World's Most Famous Office Building is not only restored to the original Art Deco intent of its creators, but is also the leader in energy efficiency in the existing built environment and modern host to major international corporations and private businesses. We are not only a link to the past, but a bridge to the future...we are still an example for others around the world to follow.

Once again, thank you for visiting and welcome to the Empire State Building!

Peter L. Malkin
Empire State Building Company L.L.C.

EMPIRE STATE BUILDING

Table of Contents

In Brief

Highlights

Soaring more than a quarter of a mile above the heart of Manhattan, the Empire State Building is the World's Most Famous Office Building. A symbol of dreams and aspirations, the Empire State Building connects with people around the world. A beacon for international and domestic tourists alike, the Empire State Building is a New York City and a National Historic Landmark.

Our world-famous 86th and 102nd floor Observatories offer unmatched views of New York City and on a clear day one can see to New Jersey, Connecticut, Massachusetts, Pennsylvania and Delaware. 1,050 feet above the city's bustling streets, the 86th floor Observatory offers panoramic views from within a glass-enclosed pavilion and from the surrounding open-air promenade. 200 feet higher, our 102nd floor Observatory is a private and serene perch in the middle of the greatest city in the world.

Our Observatories have been a "must visit" for millions each year since they opened to the public in 1931. Approximately four million people annually are whisked to our 86th and 102nd floors, consistently one of New York City's top tourist attractions. Visit our Observatories 365 days per year, day and night, rain or shine, for magnificent views of Manhattan and beyond. We are open from 8:00 a.m. to 2:00 a.m. The last elevators go up at 1:15 a.m.

The Empire State Building embodies the feeling and spirit of New York City. It is recognized not only as an iconic landmark offering some of the most spectacular views on earth, but also as an international symbol of shared hopes, dreams, and accomplishments.

PAGE 4: The ceiling murals in the lobby of ESB represent the celestial sky executed in homage to the mechanical age using aluminum and 23-karat gold leaf. TOP LEFT: Observatory visitors are welcomed to ESB's Fifth Avenue lobby every day from 8:00 a.m. to 2:00 a.m. Most tourists stop to photograph the wall mural. TOP RIGHT: The scale model, built 1/16 inch to one foot and fitted with L.E.D. lights, on display next to the Information Desk was completed in 2010 and replaced the original from 1938. BOTTOM: At the Information Desk in the Fifth Avenue lobby, staff is available to answer questions or provide directions for visitors.

TOP: A view to the northeast,
ESB is bathed in afternoon light
amidst the Citigroup, MetLife, and
Chrysler Buildings. BOTTOM:
Art Deco details are everywhere
inside and outside ESB.

Vital Statistics

- 1,050 feet to the 86th floor Observatory

- 1,250 feet to the 102nd floor Observatory

- 1,453 feet, 8 9/16 inches to the tip of the broadcast tower

- Broadcast tower adds 203 feet, 8 9/16 inches

- 103 floors

- 1,872 steps to the 103rd floor

- Sits on 79,288 square feet, approximately two acres

- Weighs 365,000 tons

- Volume is 37 million cubic feet

- 200,000 cubic feet of Indiana limestone and granite exterior cladding

- An estimated ten million bricks were used in construction

- 730 tons of aluminum and stainless steel were used in construction

- 57,000 tons of steel were used in construction

- Contains 473 miles of electrical wiring and 70 miles of pipe

- 6,514 windows

- 210 columns at the base support the entire weight of the building

- Construction was completed in one year and 45 days

- Seven million man-hours went into constructing the Empire State Building

- Final cost of property and construction was $41 million

- 73 elevators

- Five entrances

- 2.85 million rentable square feet

On Air

Broadcasting from the Empire State Building started before the building was finished, when NBC broadcast on Christmas Eve 1930. On the Empire State Building's opening night, May 1, 1931, NBC broadcast the RKO Theatre of the Air from the 86th floor. Radio programs included NBC's Mobil Oil Concert Hour, WOR's Manhattan Melodies and The Microphone in the Sky. Television debuted when NBC sent its first experimental television signal from the top of the building on December 22, 1931, and in 1939, the first regular television broadcasts began with the opening day ceremonies at the New York World's Fair. From the 1940s, popular programs like Howdy Doody were broadcast.

On July 25, 1950, New York City Mayor William O'Dwyer, RCA Chairman David Sarnoff, and other dignitaries drove the first rivets into the base of the Empire State Building's broadcast tower.

Today, the Empire State Building is the center of the New York City Tri-State region's broadcasting operations. Its technology supports delivery of broadcasting signals to cable and satellite systems, and directly to television and radio receivers, reaching over 7.4 million TV households—over 6.5% of all TV households in the U.S. More than 130 antennas provide a variety of point-to-point radio and data communications services to utility companies, telecommunications providers and public safety agencies.

Work Place

The Empire State Building is the World's Most Famous Office Building and large enough to have its own zip code—10118, which went into effect more than thirty years ago. But one does not even need the address for mail delivery—merely the recipient's name, and Empire State Building has seen letters delivered from around the world!

Workers enter through any of the five entrances. More than 64 passenger elevators service the 75 floors that house offices. State-of-the-art security allows tenants to pre-register their guests from their own computers for speedy processing and check-in at the Visitor Reception Desk in the 34th Street lobby corridor. Tenant work service requests do not even require a phone call—they are all handled over the internet.

The Empire State Building is a model of energy efficiency, with a world leading retrofit, which has established a replicable program for buildings around the world to copy (www.esbsustainability.com and pages 29-31 of this book). The World's Most Famous Office Building will also be one of the world's most energy efficient office buildings.

PAGE 8: Originally intended as a dirigible docking station, ESB's mast is now topped with a broadcast tower. As the industry leader in radio and television broadcasting, ESB is home to 34 radio and television stations that take advantage of its superior height to reach maximum audiences with both analog and digital signals. It also has the largest FM combiner system in the Western Hemisphere. TOP: The 34th Street lobby Visitor Reception Desk welcomes office tenant visitors and features internet based pre-registration technology. BOTTOM: The 34th and 33rd Street lobbies are primarily used by office tenants and their visitors.

Neighborhood Vibe

The Empire State Building is conveniently located just blocks from Pennsylvania Station, Grand Central Terminal, the Port Authority Bus Terminal, PATH trains, 18 different subway lines, and the Crosstown and Fifth Avenue buses.

Located on the 34th Street corridor, the heart of commerce and shopping in Midtown Manhattan, the Empire State Building anchors a vibrant neighborhood with world-class shopping, dining, sports, entertainment and events.

Whether starting or ending your visit to our neighborhood, there is a full day's worth of shopping between the Empire State Building and Herald Square. Macy's Herald Square is the largest department store in America and covers an entire city block with ten and one-half levels.

34th Street is filled with national and international brand stores offering something for every style and taste, for women, men, teens, and children—all within walking distance. And there is everything from convenience shopping to elegant evening cocktails right in the building.

Herald Square and Greeley Square feature pedestrian promenades with open-air seating, bringing a touch of café culture to the heart of Manhattan, just a short walk from the World's Most Famous Office Building at the very center of New York City. The award-winning gardens provide a lush spot to take a break for shoppers, office workers and tourists alike.

TOP: In busy Herald Square, on Broadway between 34th and 35th Street, is Macy's Herald Square, one of the world's largest department stores. BOTTOM: ESB anchors the 34th Street neighborhood and is part of a thriving retail district. PAGE 11: ESB's tower lights serve as a beacon to the bustling neighborhood it overlooks. In this photo, the tower lights are pink, pink and white in honor of Breast Cancer Awareness.

Evolution over Time

1799: The City of New York sells a virgin tract (now bounded by Broadway and Sixth Avenue on the west, Madison Avenue on the east, 33rd Street on the south and 36th Street on the north) for $2,600 to John Thompson for farming.

1862: William Backhouse Astor builds his mansion next door at the southwest corner of Fifth Avenue and 34th Street.

1893: William Waldorf Astor, son of John Jacob Astor, Jr., razes his inherited mansion and erects the Waldorf Hotel on the corner of Fifth Avenue and 33rd Street.

1929: John Jakob Raskob (former General Motors executive), Coleman du Pont, Pierre S. du Pont, Louis G. Kaufman and Ellis P. Earle, form Empire State, Inc. and name Alfred E. Smith, former Governor of New York to head the corporation.

1945: A B-25 Bomber crashes into the 79th floor of ESB during heavy fog on a Saturday morning. The building's construction limits the spread of fire and despite a 20-foot gash, the Empire State Building is open for business-as-usual on Monday.

1950: ESB gets an antenna tower that is over 200 feet tall.

1955: The American Society of Civil Engineers selects ESB as one of the seven greatest engineering achievements in America's history.

1956: As a symbol of welcome and freedom to visitors, four large beacon lights are installed at the foot of the tower known as "The Freedom Lights."

1962: A crew of 30 men clean the exterior of ESB for the first time since its opening. It takes about six months to complete the job.

1964: Floodlights replace the beacons, and are installed to illuminate ESB in honor of the New York World's Fair.

1825: Thompson sells the farm to Charles Lawton for $10,000.

1827: William Backhouse Astor, the second son of John Jacob Astor, buys the farm for $20,500 as an investment.

1859: John Jacob Astor, Jr. erects a mansion on the northwest corner of Fifth Avenue and 33rd Street.

1897: Mrs. William Backhouse Astor razes her mansion at Fifth Avenue and 34th Street and the Astoria Hotel is erected on the site. The new complex is known as the Waldorf Astoria Hotel.

1928: The Waldorf Astoria Hotel is sold to Bethlehem Engineering Corporation for an estimated $20 million.

1930: On March 17, construction of the Empire State Building begins. Under the direction of architects Shreve, Lamb & Harmon Associates, the framework rises 4 ½ stories per week.

1931: On May 1, President Hoover presses a button in Washington, D.C. officially opening and turning on the Empire State Building's lights.

1933: The movie *King Kong* is released in New York City on March 2.

1951: The John J. Raskob estate sells the building for $34 million to a syndicate including Roger I. Stevens and the Chicago Crown family who immediately sell the building to Prudential Insurance Company of America for $17 million, which then enters into a long-term ground lease with the Stevens syndicate.

1961: August 23, Lawrence A. Wien, Peter L. Malkin, and Harry B. Helmsley buy the building for $65 million. The price, which does not include the land, is the highest ever paid for a single building.

1966: The manually operated high-speed elevators on the first 80 floors of the building are refit for automatic operation.

1973: The tower lights are "shut off" temporarily in November in response to the energy crisis. The tower lights are not turned on again until July 3, 1974.

1976: The Empire State Building Observatory welcomes its 50 millionth visitor.

1976: To honor the United States Bicentennial, ESB installs colored floodlights to illuminate the building at night, lighting up in red, white and blue, leading to today's very popular Lighting Partners program.

1981: On May 18, the New York City Landmarks Preservation Commission declares the building a Landmark.

1982: On December 20, the Empire State Building is listed on the State and National Register of Historic Places.

1993: 6,514 ESB windows are replaced in the biggest window replacement ever authorized by the Landmarks Preservation Commission, and frames are installed in the building's original distinctive red.

2002: ESB Associates, led by Peter L. Malkin and Anthony E. Malkin, which already owned the 114-year lease on the building, purchased the land. For the first time since 1951, ownership of the land and the building are united.

2004: The tower lights are dimmed for 15 minutes to mark the death of actress Fay Wray, who starred in the 1933 movie *King Kong*.

2007: The Empire State Building is ranked number one on the list of America's Favorite Architecture by the American Institute of Architects.

2009: September 29, the newly renovated ceiling in the ESB lobby is unveiled. The renovation takes longer to complete than the original construction of the building.

1978: February 15 marks the inaugural Empire State Building Annual Run-Up.

1980: The Empire State Building gets its own zip code: 10118.

1986: The Empire State Building is recognized as a National Historic Landmark by the National Parks Services, U.S. Department of the Interior and a commemorative plaque is awarded.

1994: On February 14, the first Valentine's Day weddings take place at ESB. More than 220 couples have exchanged their vows during the event since its inception. The annually televised event is covered by news outlets around the globe.

1999-2000: More than twenty miles of fiber-optics as well as copper cabling is installed during a telecom retrofit of ESB.

2006: ESB celebrates its 75th anniversary and ownership presents a plan for the $550 million Empire State ReBuilding program, including a complete restoration and recreation of ESB's landmarked, Art Deco masterpiece lobby and the faithful recreation of the original gold and aluminum ceiling.

2009: April 5, ESB announces a groundbreaking integrated energy efficiency retrofit program, offering an internationally applicable template for retrofitting existing buildings for energy efficiency with resulting carbon footprint reduction. The team is comprised of Clinton Climate Initiative, Johnson Controls Inc., Jones Lang LaSalle and Rocky Mountain Institute. (www. esbsustainability.com)

2010: The Building Owners and Managers Association of Greater New York names the Empire State Building as 2010 Pinnacle award winner for the Historical Building of the Year.

2010: ESB earns an "Energy Star" rating from the EPA and the U.S. Department of Energy, marking it as one of the most energy efficient buildings in the United States.

Building an Icon

Bold Plans

The men who dared to dream of building the tallest skyscraper in the world were legendary in their own rights. Behind the bold plans and the vision was John Jakob Raskob, a former executive with General Motors, and the right hand man of Pierre S. du Pont. In 1928, he was pressured to resign from GM when he became chairman for the Democratic National Committee. Raskob left politics when Republican Herbert Hoover won the presidential election in 1928 over the Democratic nominee, Alfred E. Smith. Raskob cashed in his GM stock and considered what to do next. He focused on outdoing his former competitor, Walter Chrysler, whose building was on its way to being the world's tallest.

Photo credit: Avery Architectural and Fine Arts Library, Columbia University

Raskob formed a group of investors for the challenge to surpass the Chrysler Building. He convinced Al Smith, former New York Governor and recently defeated candidate in the presidential election, to join the team as President of Empire State, Inc. They purchased the Waldorf Astoria Hotel property at Fifth Avenue and 34th Street.

Architects Shreve, Lamb & Harmon were hired. Richmond Harold Shreve was the business head of the firm, William Lamb was the designer of record and Arthur Loomis Harmon was also a designer for the firm.

Starrett Brothers & Eken were known as the premier "skyline builders" of the 1920s and were chosen as the general contractors.

Photo credit: Bettman/Corbis

The announcement of the Empire State Building was made on August 29, 1929. The ambitious completion date was set for May 1, 1931.

Photo credit: Bettman/Corbis

Perfect Timing

The Empire State Building was planned during the economic boom of the 1920s, during which real estate was one of the primary economic drivers.

Skyscrapers were made possible by innovations like the electric elevator, advances in engineering, the use of structural steel, and advances in heating, ventilation, air conditioning and electrical systems. The process of making steel was perfected by 1860 and by the 1880s architects began using it to frame buildings. Otis Elevator Company installed the first successful electric elevator in 1899.

Zoning regulations at the time required setbacks from the street and directly influenced the design of the building.

The stock market crashed in 1929 and the Empire State Building was constructed when the world economy faced great uncertainty. It created thousands of jobs as contractors recruited the elite of the city's construction trades. Ultimately, upon completion, the economies of the world commenced a decline into the Great Depression.

Photo credit: Bettman/Corbis

PAGE 16 TOP: John Jakob Raskob formed a group of investors to finance the construction of the tallest skyscraper in the world, the Empire State Building. PAGE 16 CENTER: Former New York Governor Al Smith was hired to serve as President of Empire State Corporation. He is pictured in his office at ESB. PAGE 16 BOTTOM: Pictured are some of the Board of Directors of the Empire State Corporation on the site of the future Empire State Building. Left to right: Col. Michael Friedsam, John J. Raskob, Ellis P. Earle, Louis G. Kaufman, Al Smith and Robert C. Brown. TOP: The framework for ESB on April 21, 1930. BOTTOM: Former Governor Alfred E. Smith laying the cornerstone of ESB. Seventy-five stories of the steel framework of the structure have been completed.

Quick Rise to the Top

Records were broken in the construction speed of the Empire State Building. Time was of the essence and Starrett Brothers & Eken used the technique of fast-track construction—overlapping some of the work phases. The construction process began even before demolition of the Waldorf Astoria Hotel was completed.

Each part of the building process ran concurrently in order to maximize efficiency. Materials handling was a model of efficiency. Shipments went directly from the manufacturer to the job site. A railway system was built on every floor of the building to deliver materials where they were needed.

At the peak of construction 3,439 men worked on the site and the building rose at a rate of about four-and-a-half floors per week.

While the outside of the building was constructed, electricians and plumbers worked on the interior of the building.

The building was completed April 11, 1931—under budget and ahead of schedule. The Empire State Building officially opened on May 1, 1931.

TOP: Workers unload steel beams from a truck at ESB. The beams are hoisted up to the floor where they are needed. BOTTOM: Perched high above the city, the steelworkers earned the nickname "sky boys." PAGE 19 TOP: As the bolts get red hot, the heater tosses them to the riveters. PAGE 19 BOTTOM: The catcher uses a tin scoop to catch the red hot bolt, the bucker-up holds the rivet in place and the riveter uses his pneumatic gun to drive the bolt home.

The Sky Boys

Lewis Wickes Hine's photographs recorded the men who built the building, capturing their courage, skill and determination. Architect Richmond Shreve was Hine's neighbor and recommended him for the job of photographing the construction of the building from March 1930 to May 1931. Hine climbed out on the steel beams, taking some of the same chances as the workers. Always resourceful, he fashioned a basket of sorts and swung out in it to photograph the ironworkers from the perspective he wanted, sometimes 1,000 feet above the ground.

The steelworkers were the first to earn the name "sky boys" as they captivated onlookers and the press. The daring workers climbed and confidently swung out hundreds of feet in the air. The gangs of riveters also fascinated passersby as they worked in teams of four, coordinating their movements with practiced ease.

More than seven million man-hours were logged to complete the Empire State Building in less than 14 months.

New Style

Designed in the late 1920s, the Empire State Building reflects the geometric shapes and streamlined form of the Art Deco style. Art Deco infused opulence and confidence of the era with aspects of industrial design. For instance, the Empire State Building's lobby ceiling mural design is a celestial sky executed in gears and wheels in homage to the machine age. The architects used aluminum, then a technological innovation, mixed with gold to present the greatest mixture of technology and opulence.

Much of the Empire State Building's style was born from logical and simple solutions to economic and technical problems. Featuring the classical composition of a five-story base with a large tower, the setbacks were incorporated into the design in order to conform to New York City's 1916 zoning law. The architectural firm Shreve, Lamb & Harmon wanted the building to make a grand impression with clean, soaring lines. Legend says the design was inspired by the shape of a pencil.

Indiana limestone was chosen to cover the building exterior. The 6,514 windows and aluminum spandrels were set visually flush with the limestone facing, to give the impression of solidity. The stone was rough-cut in the quarry and placed without any final cutting or fitting. Metal strips covered the stone's edges, saving time. Chrome-nickel steel was used for mullions running from the sixth to the 85th floor. Eagles flank the main entrance.

The lobby soars thirty feet, covered with 10,000 square feet of international Rose Famosa and Estrallante marble and granite. Accents of brushed stainless steel are threaded throughout the lobby.

The Art Deco influence in the lobby design includes modern elements and materials like stainless steel and aluminum that echo the ceiling's machine-patterned interpretations of natural elements such as sunbursts and stars. The focal point in the Fifth Avenue lobby is a metal mosaic featuring the Empire State Building against an outline of the state of New York, with light beams radiating from the building.

PAGE 20: Opening Day ceremonies for ESB took place on May 1, 1931. Al Smith, President of the Empire State Corporation, stands with his two five-year-old grandchildren. This photo shows the lobby as notables wait for President Hoover to turn the lights on ceremoniously from Washington, D.C. BOTTOM LEFT: ESB soars above Manhattan. BOTTOM RIGHT: A plaque hangs in the lobby, honoring the 32 workers who received Craftsmanship Awards when the building was completed.

PAGE 20 Photo credit: Avery Architectural and Fine Arts Library, Columbia University

EMPIRE STATE CRAFTSMANSHIP AWARDS

GEORGE R. ADAMS	PAINTER AND DECORATOR
ADAM BIGELOW	DAMP PROOFER
GUS COMEDECA	STEAM SHOVEL OPERATOR
JOHN CONNOLLY	ROOFER
WILLIAM DENEEN	ELEVATOR CONSTR'S HELPER
LOUIS HUMMELL	STEAMFITTER
JAMES IRONS	STONE CUTTER
ARTHUR JONES	ORN. IRON & BRONZE WORKER
JAMES P. KERR	STONE SETTER
FRANK J. KLEIN	PLASTERER
VLADIMIR KOZLOFF	WRECKER
SAMUEL LAGINSKY	GLAZIER
JOSEPH LEFFERT	TILE SETTER'S HELPER
PETER MADDEN	ASBESTOS WORKER
R. MADDALENA	TILE SETTER
FERRUCCIO MARIUTTO	TERRAZZO WORKER
MATTHEW M. McKEAN	CARPENTER
THOMAS McWEENEY	ELEVATOR CONSTRUCTOR
FRANK MOEGLIN	SHEET METAL WORKER
WILLIAM L. MORAN	STEAM FITTER'S HELPER
JOHN E. O'CONNOR	PLUMBER
FRANK W. PIERSON, JR.	METAL LATHER
GUISEPPE RUSCIANI	LABORER
GINO SANTONI	CEMENT MASON
OWEN SCANLON	MARBLE SETTER'S HELPER
CHARLES E. SEXTON	BRICKLAYER
LOUIS SHANE, JR.	MARBLE SETTER
CLIFFORD SMITH	ELECTRICIAN
MICHAEL TIERNEY	ROCK DRILLER
PIETRO VESCOVI	TERRAZZO WORKER'S HELPER
THOMAS F. WALSH	HOISTING ENGINEER
THOMAS WALSH	DERRICKMAN

Renovation and Restoration

Over time, key design elements in the Empire State Building were obscured and lost. In the 1960s, an acrylic-panel dropped ceiling was installed, covering the original ceiling murals and introducing fluorescent lighting to the lobby. Glasswork that once lined elevator banks and side corridors was eventually replaced with acrylic inlays.

As part of the historic more than $550 million Empire State ReBuilding program launched in 2007, the Empire State Building has been restored, its Art Deco grandeur recreated, and state-of-the-art upgrades added. A team of world-class engineers, architects, contractors, artists, historians and craftsmen worked together on this once-in-a-lifetime project.

In the lobby, photographs and descriptions of original glasswork panels were discovered in museums and served as a guide for artisans to recreate over 12,000 linear feet of the historic glasswork.

Lighting
The team matched the original Empire State Building lighting plans with modern lighting technology, featuring energy-efficient bulbs and ballasts, which adjust based on lighting needs and New York City power grid demands.

As the Empire State Building restored the original 1930s lighting levels, the dramatic original vision of its designers was evident as the subtle hues and colors in the lobby's stone walls reappeared. Now, eyes are naturally drawn to the ceiling mural as the focal point for the restored lobby.

Original lobby blueprints show plans for two ornate chandeliers over the second-floor pedestrian bridges; however, the original chandeliers were never created and two 1920s fixtures were hung, likely as a cost-saving measure. The Landmarks Preservation Commission approved installation of the originally intended chandeliers, which were fabricated by Rambusch, a fourth-generation firm that created the original Empire State Building ceiling mural.

Lobby Mural
On the iconic wall mural in the Fifth Avenue main lobby, the restored anemometer (which was long ago replaced by a clock) once again measures wind speed and direction from a weather station above the 86th floor Observatory. Although the anemometer was part of the original 1930s design, its weather station offers modern-day technology, linking it to not only the main lobby, but also the Empire State Building website (www.esbnyc.com) and real-time weather dials in the Observatory areas.

BOTTOM LEFT: Over 12,000 linear feet of glasswork lining the elevator banks and side corridors matches the original 1930s design. BOTTOM RIGHT: New chandeliers were fabricated based on the original drawings used during the building's construction, completing the original design vision for the building. PAGE 23: Wind speed and direction from a weather station above the 86th floor Observatory are measured on the restored anemometer in the lobby mural. Replaced by a clock long ago, the anemometer was part of the restoration project that returned the lobby to its 1930s design.

Marble

The original masons used exquisite, carefully selected international marbles throughout the lobby to create a unique example of "bookmatching," in which slices of stone from the same block are arranged to mirror each other, highlighting the marble's natural veining for artistic purposes. Pieces of the building's original marble were removed or damaged over time, so restoration architects and trades searched the world and replaced lost material with new to match as closely as possible.

Ceiling Mural

The building's lobbies originally featured ornate ceiling murals created with aluminum and 23-karat gold leaf applied to canvas. The murals were an Art Deco representation of a celestial sky with sunbursts and stars. The ceiling remained the focal point of the lobby until the 1960s, when it was painted over and covered with an acrylic-panel dropped ceiling, and fluorescent light fixtures were installed to modernize the building's architectural aesthetic.

A team of artists and historians worked collaboratively to restore the original 1930s ceiling. Guided by historic photographs, on-site forensic analysis of dirt patterns attracted to the underlying aluminum and gold leaf, and existing architectural elements, the restoration team employed a 26-step process to recreate the Art Deco mural using the same techniques as the original artists from Rambusch Studios. The full replication, including research, design, execution and installation took approximately two years to complete at EverGreene's New York studio—it took longer to recreate the ceiling murals than the original construction of the building.

PAGE 24: Marble from as far away as Italy and as close as a warehouse in Greenpoint, Brooklyn was used to replace pieces of the building's original marble that were removed or damaged over time. PAGE 25: With the entire lobby covered in scaffolding, a team of artisans painstakingly recreated the ceiling murals using 1,300 square feet of 23-karat gold leaf and 14,000 square feet of aluminum leaf. More than 50 artists, site painters and installers worked on the project.

Observatory Experience

The 2nd floor ticketing area features flooring with a multi-colored chevron pattern with an Empire State Building logo design as a focal point. Almost 2,000 "windows" were individually cut in the design. The ticketing area also features an eye-opening, educational explanation of the groundbreaking energy efficiency program created at the Empire State Building, and reflects on its impacts when adopted more broadly by cities around the world.

The 86th floor Observatory, with its popular 360-degree outdoor deck, has indoor viewing galleries for guests to enjoy the views rain or shine, day or night. The East and West galleries have a modern Art Deco design, mixed with bold color and graphics. The gallery ceilings depict the same interpretive celestial design seen in the Empire State Building's 1930s main lobby ceiling mural.

The 102nd floor Observatory—originally planned to be the check-in area under the mooring mast for dirigible landings in 1931—is the highest point tourists can reach in the Manhattan sky, soaring 1,250 feet above the ground. The renovations on the 102nd floor included exposing the original steel beams, ladder and stairwell, and enclosing them in glass to let in natural light; replacing the windows with energy-efficient tinted glass and weather-proof panes; and carrying over the modern Art Deco design elements featured on the 86th floor.

PAGE 26 TOP: The 86th floor Observatory offers visitors unobstructed views from the indoor viewing gallery. PAGE 26 BOTTOM: The renovated 102nd floor Observatory provides visitors with the highest view of the city accessible to tourists. LEFT: Attentive ESB employees guide visitors and stand watch in uniforms inspired by original designs of the 1930s. TOP RIGHT: An Empire State Building rendition is a focal point in welcoming visitors to the 2nd floor ticketing area. BOTTOM RIGHT: The expanded 3,000 square-foot gift shop offers a broad range of mementos, including many available only at ESB.

New Icon of Sustainability

Built during the Great Depression, the Empire State Building is the World's Most Famous Office Building. Today the building has completed a major energy efficiency retrofit and has incorporated a suite of green practices to become the leading example of redevelopment with environmental awareness. The Empire State Building is retrofitted for the next century through a replicable, groundbreaking process to improve energy efficiency, indoor environmental quality, and reduce its carbon footprint, making it one of the most energy efficient buildings in the world.

Starting in February 2008, consulting, design and construction partners Clinton Climate Initiative, Johnson Controls Inc., Jones Lang LaSalle and Rocky Mountain Institute worked as a seamless team, creating a replicable model that demonstrates the business case for integrated energy efficient retrofits in the existing built environment with short term payback. This process, which includes rigorous energy modeling and financial analysis, has resulted in the implementation of eight energy efficiency projects at the Empire State Building. These projects reduce the building's energy consumption of watts and BTUs by a guaranteed 38% (the guarantee only covers 90% of the savings, so actual savings are anticipated to exceed 40% and $4.4 million annually, with a recoupment of expense in three years.)

The sustainability retrofit considered 67 different energy efficiency measures before agreeing on eight key steps. The Empire State Building has become a laboratory visited by engineers, lawmakers, academics, and other property owners and managers. The retrofit provides a non-proprietary, open-sourced replicable model for similar projects around the world and stands as a global example of what can be achieved.

The building systems work will result in over 55% of the projected energy savings. The balance of the work in tenant spaces will be finished by the end of 2013.

The biggest single source of carbon emissions throughout the world is the energy used in buildings. In New York City, buildings consume 80% of all energy. According to NYC's Mayor's Office of Long Term Planning, 20% of the buildings consume 80% of that energy, or 64% of the total. Applying the 40% savings achieved at the Empire State Building to NYC will result in a 25% reduction of total New York City energy consumption.

The Empire State Building model will stimulate economic growth, innovation and job creation while at the same time providing a measurable payback financially and environmentally.

The retrofit has attracted like-minded tenants such as Skanska, one of the world's leading construction groups, who moved their USA headquarters to the Empire State Building's 32nd floor. Skanska is the first tenant to earn LEED (Leadership in Energy and Environmental Design) for Commercial Interiors Platinum certification—the highest certification level possible—in the Empire State Building. All new office installations in the Empire State Building protect tenants from energy cost increases through proven efficiency.

PAGE 28: ESB is a leading example of innovative building management, as it undergoes a retrofit to improve energy efficiency and financial performance. BOTTOM: Former President William J. Clinton speaks about ESB's sustainability retrofit underway and Clinton Climate Initiative's participation in the project. Anthony Malkin of the Empire State Building Company is seated on the right.

Adding it all up

The Empire State Building is guaranteed to repay the additional $13 million cost added to the building's upgrade program in about three years, and will see an annual energy savings of $4.4 million and cut its overall energy consumption by 38% primarily through eight key projects.

1.

Windows:

Typical single or double pane windows provide very little insulation and protection against solar heat gain—leading to large heating and cooling loads. This project involved upgrading 6,514 windows at the Empire State Building. Each window was removed and "remanufactured" within the building. The remanufacturing involved the insertion of a thin film and gaseous mixture between the existing two panes of glass and brings down the overall energy use by reducing heat loss or gains between the outside and inside of the building. 96% of the original glass and frames were reused.

SAVINGS
CO2 1,150 tons/yr
ENERGY 11.4M kBtu/yr
COSTS $410K/yr

5%

2.

Radiator Insulation Retrofit:

One steam radiator is located beneath each of the 6,514 windows at the Empire State Building. Previously, nearly half the heat from the radiator went into the building, while the other half escaped through the wall. This project involved the installation of "radiative barriers" behind each of the radiators to ensure most of the heat goes into the building instead of out into the New York air.

SAVINGS
CO2 480 tons/yr
ENERGY 6.9M kBtu/yr
COSTS $190K/yr

3%

3.

Lighting, Daylighting and Plug Upgrades:

Office buildings use a huge amount of energy providing artificial light even on sunny days. This project includes maximizing daylighting and designing more efficient lighting and lighting controls for tenant spaces. It also addresses tenant plug load energy use (computers, monitors, coffee makers, etc.) by providing plug load occupancy sensors.

SAVINGS
CO2 2,060 tons/yr
ENERGY 13.7M kBtu/yr
COSTS $941K/yr

6%

4.

Air Handler Replacements:

Replacing over 300 existing air handling units with newer, and fewer, more efficient units. The new digital variable air volume units will be easier to maintain, provide greater occupant comfort and save more energy.

SAVINGS
CO2 1,520 tons/yr
ENERGY 11.4M kBtu/yr
COSTS $703K/yr

5%

5.

Chiller Plant Retrofit:

With more efficient, better insulated windows, the cooling needs of the building are greatly reduced. So instead of installing new chillers or replacing the existing chillers, the Empire State Building retrofitted four of its existing electric chillers. The shells of each of the chillers were reused, while the "guts" (tubes, valves, motors, etc.) were removed and replaced. This retrofit dramatically improved the energy efficiency and controllability of the electric chillers.

SAVINGS
CO2 1,430 tons/yr
ENERGY 11.4M kBtu/yr
COSTS $676K/yr

5%

6.

Whole-Building Control System Upgrade:

Upgrading existing and installing new building controls helped to optimize the HVAC operation as well as provide more detailed sub-metering of electricity use. It is the largest wireless building control system in the world and provides continuous real-time data to the operators of the Empire State Building.

SAVINGS
CO2 1,900 tons/yr
ENERGY 20.6M kBtu/yr
COSTS $741K/yr

9%

7.

Ventilation Control Upgrade:

New York City building code requires delivery of fresh air to occupied spaces, ensuring adequate air quality. CO2 sensors will modulate the amount of outside air in occupied spaces based on number of occupants. Cool exterior air will be brought in and cleaned by filters—saving on the building's chiller plant operation while improving indoor air quality. Everything is controlled by integrated, digital, building energy management systems, saving energy and creating a healthier work environment.

SAVINGS
CO2 300 tons/yr
ENERGY 4.6M kBtu/yr
COSTS $117K/yr

2%

8.

Tenant Energy Management Systems:

One of the first steps in reducing loads is getting a better understanding of how energy is currently used. The tenant energy management program engages existing tenants in the building's sustainability efforts to realize energy savings over the next several years. With sub-metering, tenants are able to access accurate and transparent energy use data online as well as benchmark themselves against other tenants and obtain real-time energy savings and sustainability tips.

SAVINGS
CO2 743 tons/yr
ENERGY 6.9M kBtu/yr
COSTS $387K/yr

3%

The eight projects will save 105,000 metric tons of carbon dioxide over the next 15 years. This is equivalent to taking more than 19,000 cars off the road.

Views from Above

The Empire State Building's 86th and 102nd floor Observatories offer unmatched views of New York City and beyond. People travel from all over the world to look out upon New York from its very center. The Observatories of the Empire State Building are open from 8 a.m. to 2 a.m. seven days a week. Tickets can be purchased on site or online at www.esbnyc.com.

The spectacular 360-degree view of the Big Apple and the metropolitan area are explained in an optional audio tour, which is available in seven different languages. To complement the audio tour and provide visitors close-up views of what is described, powerful binoculars are available on the outside deck of the 86th floor Observatory.

On a clear day, visitors can see into New Jersey, Delaware, Pennsylvania, Connecticut and Massachusetts. The Statue of Liberty, Central Park, the Flatiron Building and the Chrysler Building highlight the panoramic view. One of the best times to visit the Observatories is at night. The view shimmering with light is one of the most romantic views of the city. As an added bonus, the lines are shorter at night.

TOP RIGHT: The distinctive spire of the Chrysler Building stands out in the view northeast from the 86th floor Observatory. BOTTOM: ESB's Observatory on the 86th floor offers glittering night views of New York City. The view west shows the Hudson River shining darkly and New Jersey on its far side. PAGE 35: The Financial District is at the southern tip of Manhattan in the view south from ESB. The Statue of Liberty and adjacent Ellis Island are visible on the right of the picture.

East

Directly east is the Borough of Queens, separated from Manhattan by the East River. Just before the river stands the green glass of the United Nations Headquarters, and to its left is the famed Chrysler Building. Across the river, standing above all of Queens, is the Citigroup Building. Keep spanning the river and you'll see two bridges: the Queensborough Bridge (also known as the 59th Street Bridge), which connects Queens and Manhattan, and the Robert F. Kennedy Bridge, which connects Queens, Manhattan, and The Bronx. Look carefully and you can see planes taking off and landing at LaGuardia and Kennedy Airports.

West

The jet-black spike with the red "1" at its top is One Penn Plaza, which rises to the right and above the famous sports arena Madison Square Garden. Immediately to the right, all the way by the Hudson River, is the Jacob Javits Convention Center. Just beyond is the former WWII aircraft carrier *Intrepid*; it is home to the Sea, Air and Space Museum. To the right, the square building with the spire is the New York Times building. Across the Hudson is New Jersey, and beyond that is Pennsylvania's Pocono Mountains and Delaware.

South

What you'll notice immediately is Manhattan's Wall Street district. But just before you get all the way downtown, you can see the aptly named Flatiron Building just on the other side of Madison Square Park, and then the historic Woolworth Building, once the world's tallest at just 60 floors. Look to the right and you'll see the same sight that greeted countless numbers of U.S. immigrants: the Statue of Liberty and Ellis Island. Just beyond, the Verrazano Bridge over the entrance to New York Harbor. To the lower left, check out two classics: the Manhattan and Brooklyn bridges.

North

From the left to the right, start with the Hudson River; watch it as it flows beneath the majestic George Washington Bridge, which connects New York to New Jersey. You will see the green MetLife Building, directly in front of One Bryant Park with its angles and spire. Moving right, there is the GE Building, the angled roof of Citigroup Center, and the second MetLife Building. If it's a clear day, you can see well beyond New York and New Jersey to Connecticut, and even Massachusetts.

PAGE 38-39: Visitors from all over the world and all walks of life enjoy the view from the 86th floor Observatory. The Observatory is open daily 365 days a year from 8:00 a.m. to 2:00 a.m. The last elevators go up at 1:15 a.m. An audio tour is available in seven different languages to complement visitors' experience.

In Movies and on Television

Starring Roles

The Empire State Building captures the imagination of filmmakers around the world and has played a role in film and television for almost 80 years, earning its status as an international pop culture icon. One of the Empire State Building's earliest appearances was in the classic 1933 movie *King Kong* starring Fay Wray. King Kong climbs up to the spire to try to escape his attackers, with the screaming Fay Wray in his grasp.

The unforgettable 1957 tragic love story, *An Affair to Remember,* starred Cary Grant and Deborah Kerr and was nominated for four Oscars. The story begins with a couple who fall in love and agree to meet in six months at the Empire State Building. Terry (played by actress Deborah Kerr) says that the Observation Deck at Empire State Building is as close as one can get to heaven in New York City.

Another famous meeting on top of the Empire State Building was featured in the romantic comedy, *Sleepless In Seattle,* starring Tom Hanks and Meg Ryan (and the Empire State Building Observatory was the site of a missed meeting in *Gossip Girl*). Empire State Building played prominent roles in other movie classics such as *When Harry Met Sally, Independence Day, Last Action Hero,* and *Taxi Driver*.

BOTTOM LEFT: In this 1933 *King Kong* movie poster Kong fights off attacking planes while holding Fay Wray. BOTTOM RIGHT: The movie poster for the 2005 remake of *King Kong* features Kong in the same precarious position as the original 1933 movie poster. PAGE 41 TOP LEFT: *Sleepless in Seattle* included a fateful meeting of the characters played by Tom Hanks and Meg Ryan at ESB's Observation Deck. PAGE 41 TOP RIGHT: The 1957 movie, *An Affair to Remember,* also featured a fateful meeting of the lead characters played by Cary Grant and Deborah Kerr.

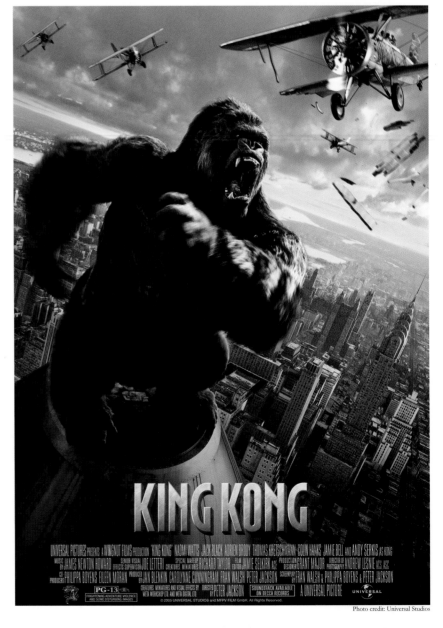

Photo credit: Universal Studios

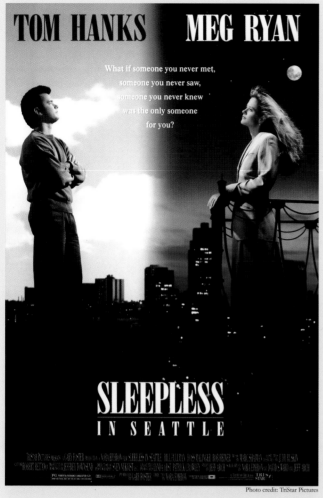

Photo credit: TriStar Pictures

Photo credit: Twentieth Century-Fox Film Corporation

In the Movies The Empire State Building appears in these movies:

Annie Hall 1977
Any Wednesday 1966
April Fools 1969
Ask Any Girl 1959
Auntie Mame 1958
Bachelor Apartment 1931
Ball of Fire 1941
Bell, Book and Candle 1959
Best of Everything 1959
Bright Lights, Big City 1988
Big City Blues 1997
Blackboard Jungle 1955
Broadway Melody 1929
Butcher's Wife 1991
Champion 1949
Charlie Chan of Broadway 1937
Come to the Stable 1949
Coogan's Bluff 1968
Daddy Long Legs 1955
Detective Story 1951
Easter Parade 1948
Edge of the City 1957
Elf 2003

Fail-Safe 1964
FBI Story 1959
Fine Madness 1966
Finian's Rainbow 1968
Footlight Serenade 1942
Fitzwilly 1967
French Connection I 1971
For Pete's Sake 1974
Funny Face 1957
French Line 1953
Garment Jungle 1957
Guys & Dolls 1955
Hancock 2008
Hatful of Rain 1957
How to Succeed in Business
   Without Really Trying 1967
I Take this Woman 1931, 1940
Independence Day 1996
Its Always Fair Weather 1955
Ivory Ape 1980
King Kong 1933, 1976, 2005
King of the Gypsies 1978
Klute 1971

Kramer vs. Kramer 1979
Last Action Hero 1993
Law & Disorder 1974
Love With a Proper Stranger 1963
Lullaby of Broadway 1951
Madigan 1968
Man in the Gray Flannel Suit 1956
Manhattan 1979
Manhattan Melodrama 1934
Moon is Blue 1953
My Man Godfrey (Remake) 1957
My Sister Eileen 1955
New York Confidential 1955
New York, New York 1977
New York Town 1941
New York Stories 1989
North By Northwest 1959
Nothing Sacred 1937
On the Town 1949
On the Waterfront 1954
Pawnbroker 1965
Percy Jackson & the Olympians:
   The Lightning Thief 2010

President's Analyst 1967
Prisoner of Second Avenue 1975
Rock Around the Clock 1956
Saboteur 1942
Saint in New York 1938
Serpico 1973
Seven Ups 1973
Shaft 1971
Sky's the Limit 1943
Slaughter on Tenth Avenue 1957
Sleepless in Seattle 1993
So This is New York 1948
Stand Up and Cheer 1934
Street Scene 1931
Sunday in New York 1963
Superman II 1981
Sweet Charity 1969
Taxi Driver 1976
When Harry Met Sally 1989
Who Done It 1942
World of Henry Orient 1964
World Flesh & Devil 1959
You Gotta Stay Happy 1948

Visiting Stars

The world's most famous people visit the Empire State Building to enjoy the unmatched view. Often arriving unannounced with their own friends and families, celebrities and dignitaries alike admire the panorama from the 86th and 102nd floor Observatories. There is a special private walkway on the second floor, which brings celebrities to the high-speed elevators for the Observation Deck, and they also can visit the private 103rd floor parapet balcony.

The iconic Empire State Building has attracted well-known people from around the globe, such as Queen Elizabeth and Prince Phillip in 1957, Fidel Castro in 1959, Nikita Khrushchev in 1959 and Pele the soccer star in 1975. Recent celebrity visitors include Yankee legend Yogi Berra, the Beach Boys, Justin Bieber, the Radio City Rockettes and Consul General Peng Keyu of the People's Republic of China.

TOP RIGHT: Pop star Kylie Minogue lights ESB in honor of the Coty-DKMS Linked Against Leukemia partnership, a charitable drive promoting bone marrow donations. BOTTOM LEFT: A private walkway for celebrities visiting ESB features a beautiful custom floor and photographs of previous celebrity visitors. BOTTOM RIGHT: Tampa Bay Ray Johnny Damon poses for a photo for NASCAR driver Jimmie Johnson on ESB's 86th floor. PAGE 43 TOP: Roger Federer poses with his 2008 U.S. Open Tennis Championship trophy on the 103rd floor at ESB. PAGE 43 BOTTOM: Golf legend Jack Nicklaus visits the 86th floor Observatory on behalf of The First Tee initiative of the World Golf Foundation.

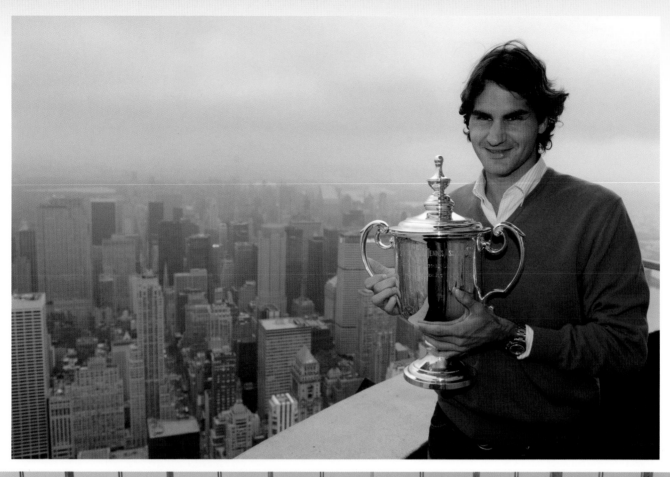

TOP: Boxing World Heavyweight Champion Wladimir Klitschko visits ESB's 86th floor Observatory. BOTTOM: Pierce Brosnan from the cast of *Percy Jackson & The Olympians: The Lightning Thief* poses for a photo on the 86th floor. PAGE 45 TOP: Jimmie Johnson, NASCAR Sprint Cup Series five-time Champion, celebrates his 2009 victory on the 103rd floor of ESB. PAGE 45 BOTTOM: In celebration of the 10th anniversary of Body by Victoria, Victoria's Secret models (L to R) Alessandra Ambrosio, Emanuela De Paula, Marisa Miller and Lindsay Ellingson posed at the Observation Deck on top of ESB.

Illuminated

The Empire State Building was lit for the first time on November 8, 1932 with a beacon visible for a 50-mile radius when Franklin D. Roosevelt was elected President of the United States. Additional lights were added when four revolving beacons called *Freedom Lights* were installed in 1956. Each beacon measured five feet in diameter and weighed one ton. Revolving in perfect synchronization, they generated 45-million candle power and were visible from 80 miles away. In 1964, the beacons were replaced with floodlights that illuminated the top 30 floors of the building for the New York World's Fair. Colored lights were added in 1976 for the Bicentennial celebration. Fluorescent lighting was added to the upper mooring mast in 1984.

There are three levels of lights and all three can light up in blue, red, green, yellow, orange, pink, purple or white. The lighting effects are not limited to a single solid color, and offer a kaleidoscope of color possibilities.

White lights represent the Empire State Building's signature lighting. The lights turn on at dusk and turn off at 2 a.m. every day. The lighting schedule is published on the Empire State Building's website: www.esbnyc.com.

Answers: 1) Empire State Building Run-Up 2) St. Patrick's Day 3) Westminster Kennel Club 4) Easter 5) Opening Day for United States Tennis Association US Open Finals Weekend 6) Subway Series (Yankees & Mets) 7) NYC Marathon 8) Valentine's Day 9) Chanukah 10) Christmas 11) 2008 Superbowl Champion, NY Giants 12) Grateful Dead exhibit at the New-York Historical Society 13) Breast Cancer Awareness 14) Halloween 15) AIDS Walk 16) 2008 Beijing Olympics (U.S. & China) 17) Heritage of Pride 18) Food Bank 19) Belmont Stakes 20) National EMS Week

46

Test your color IQ
What do the Empire State Building's light colors stand for?
Answers on page 46